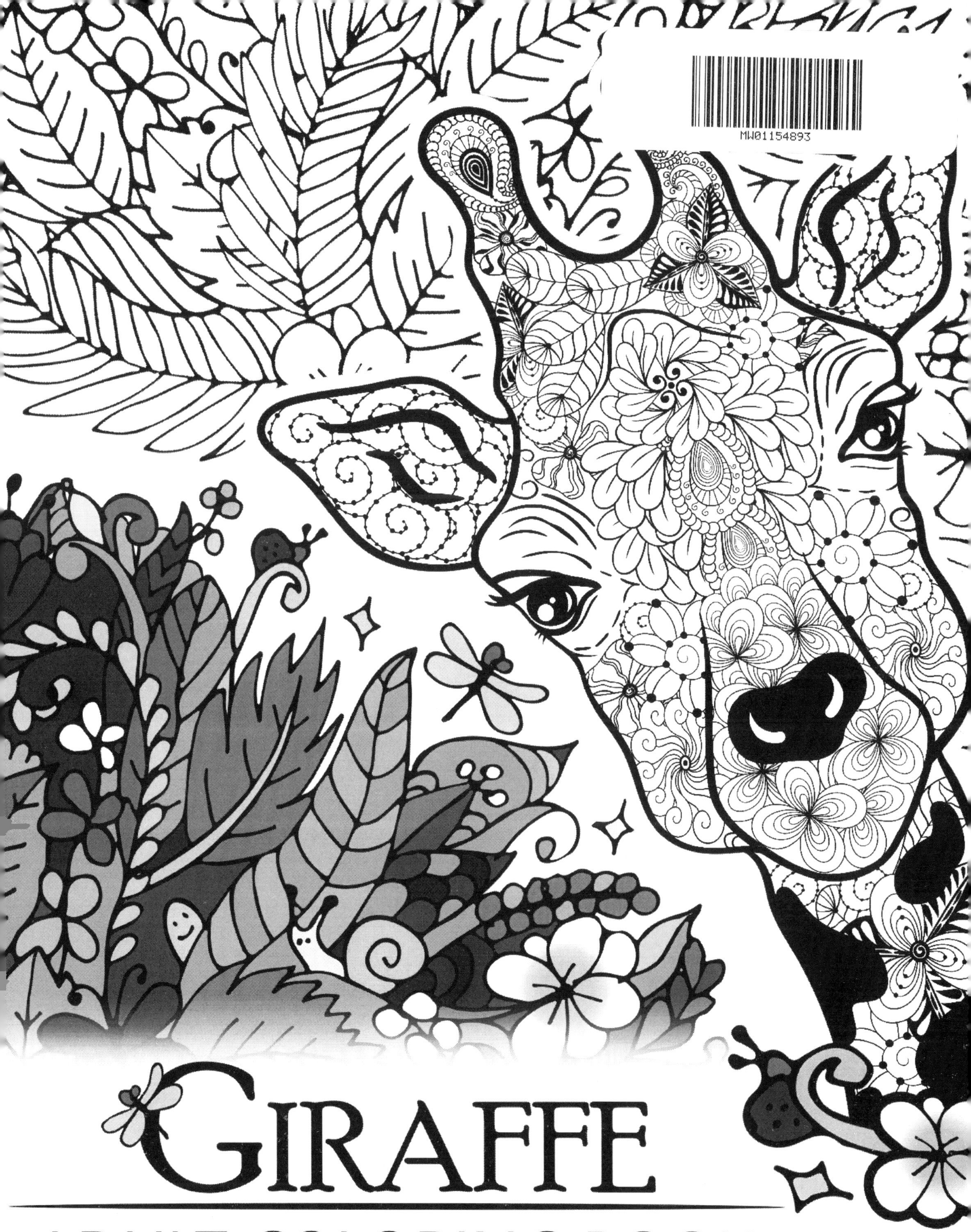

GIRAFFE

ADULT COLORING BOOK

BLUE NAVY

Printed in The U.S.A.

TEST YOUR COLOR

1.

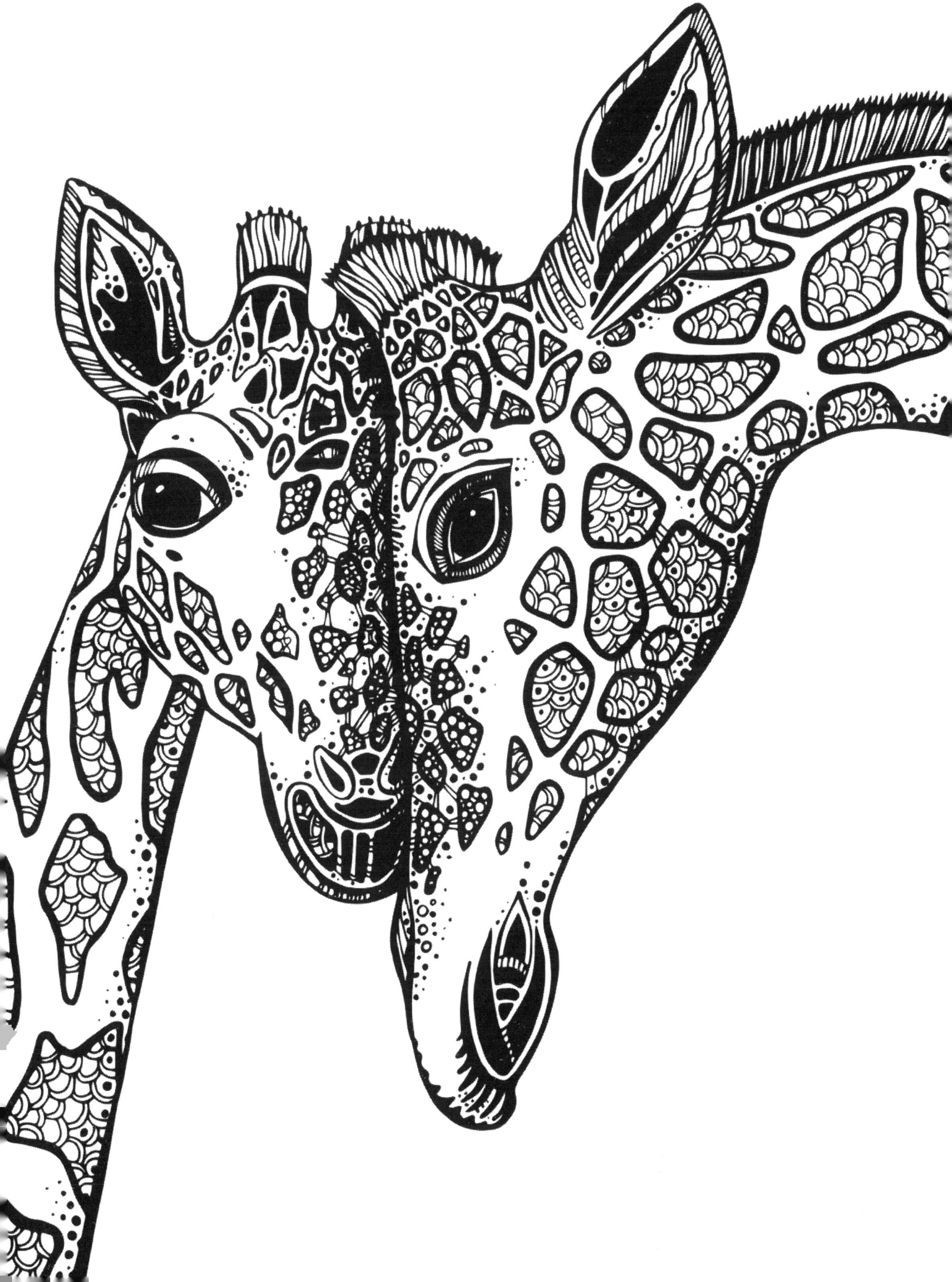

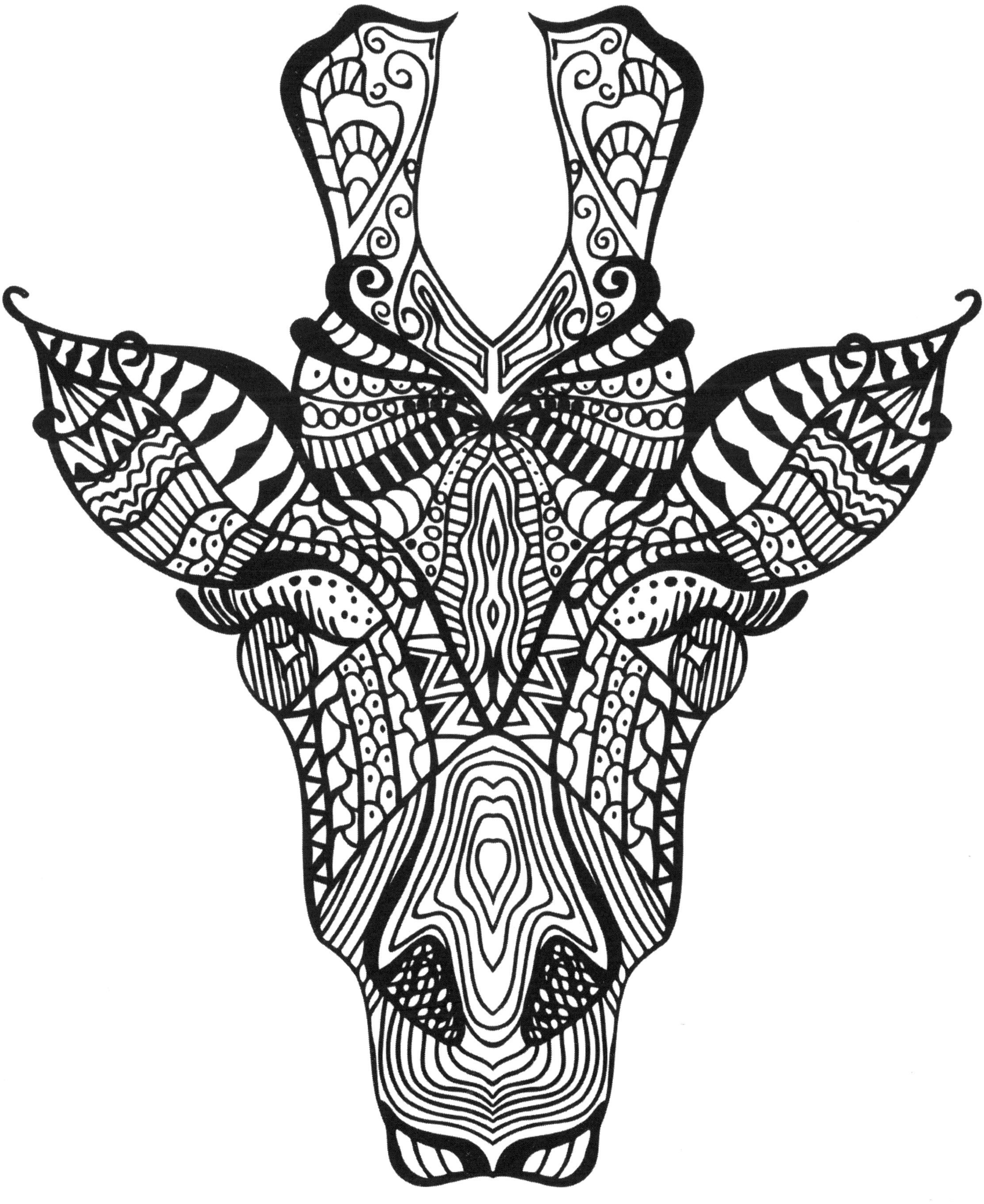

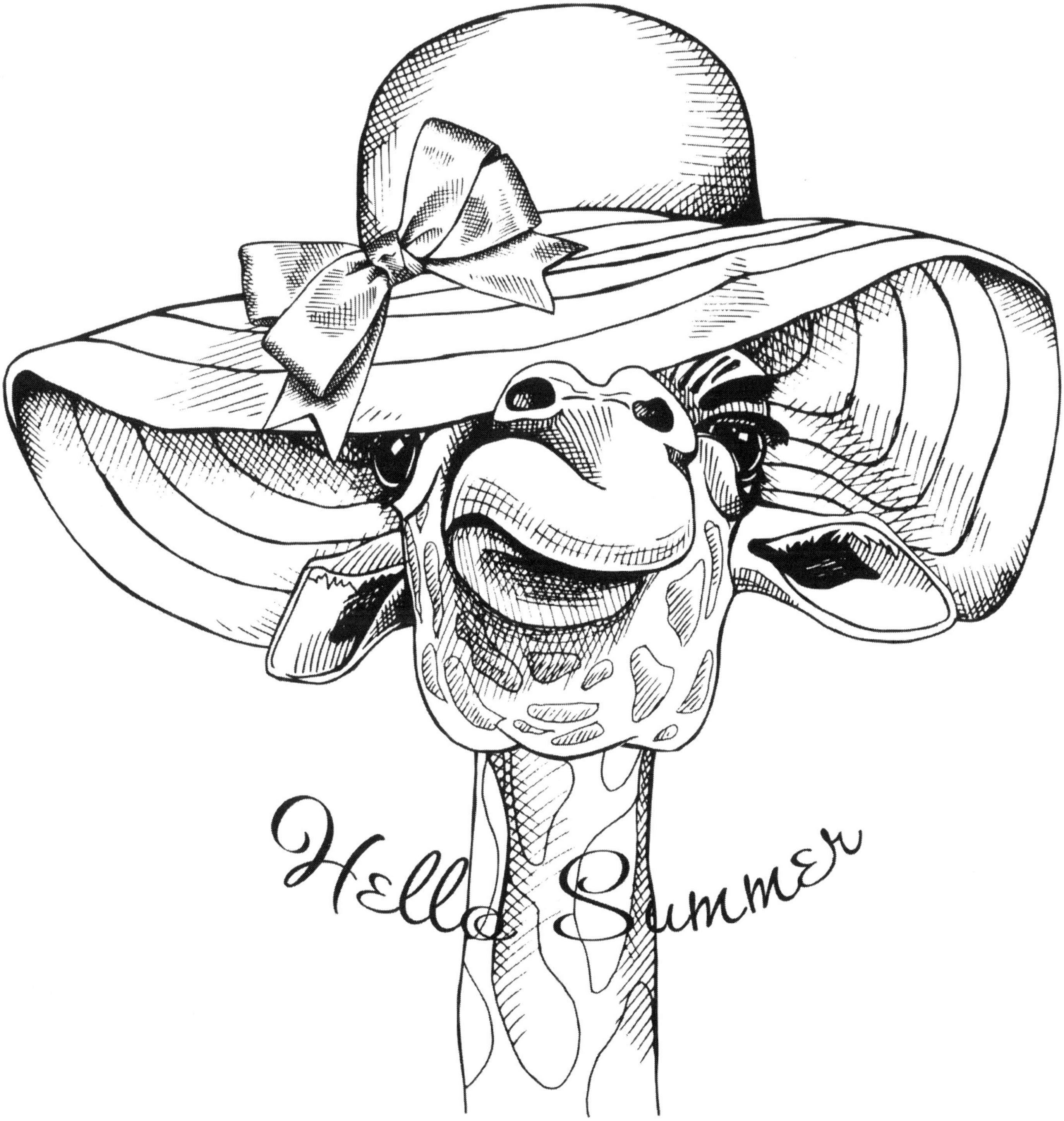
Hello Summer

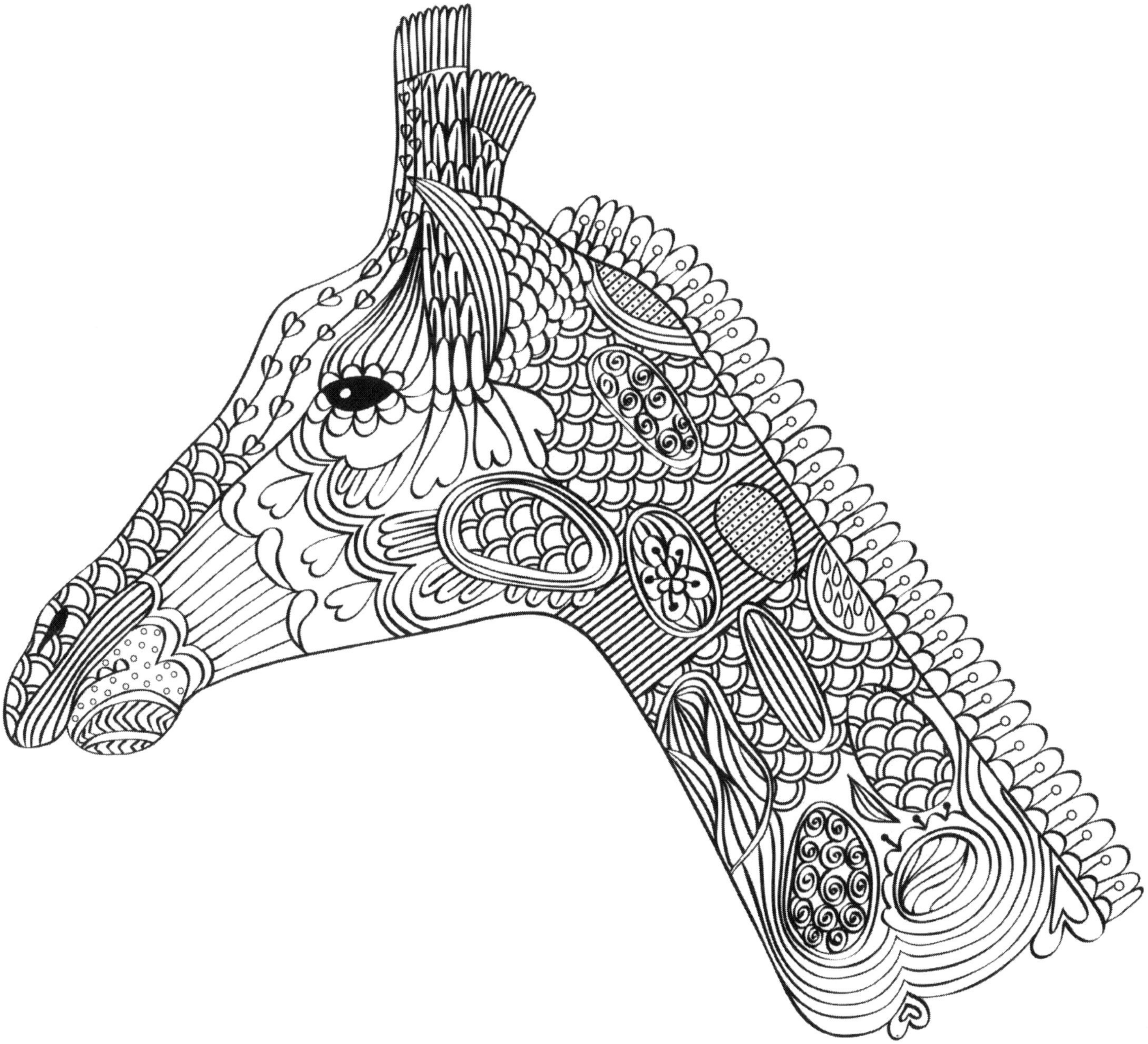

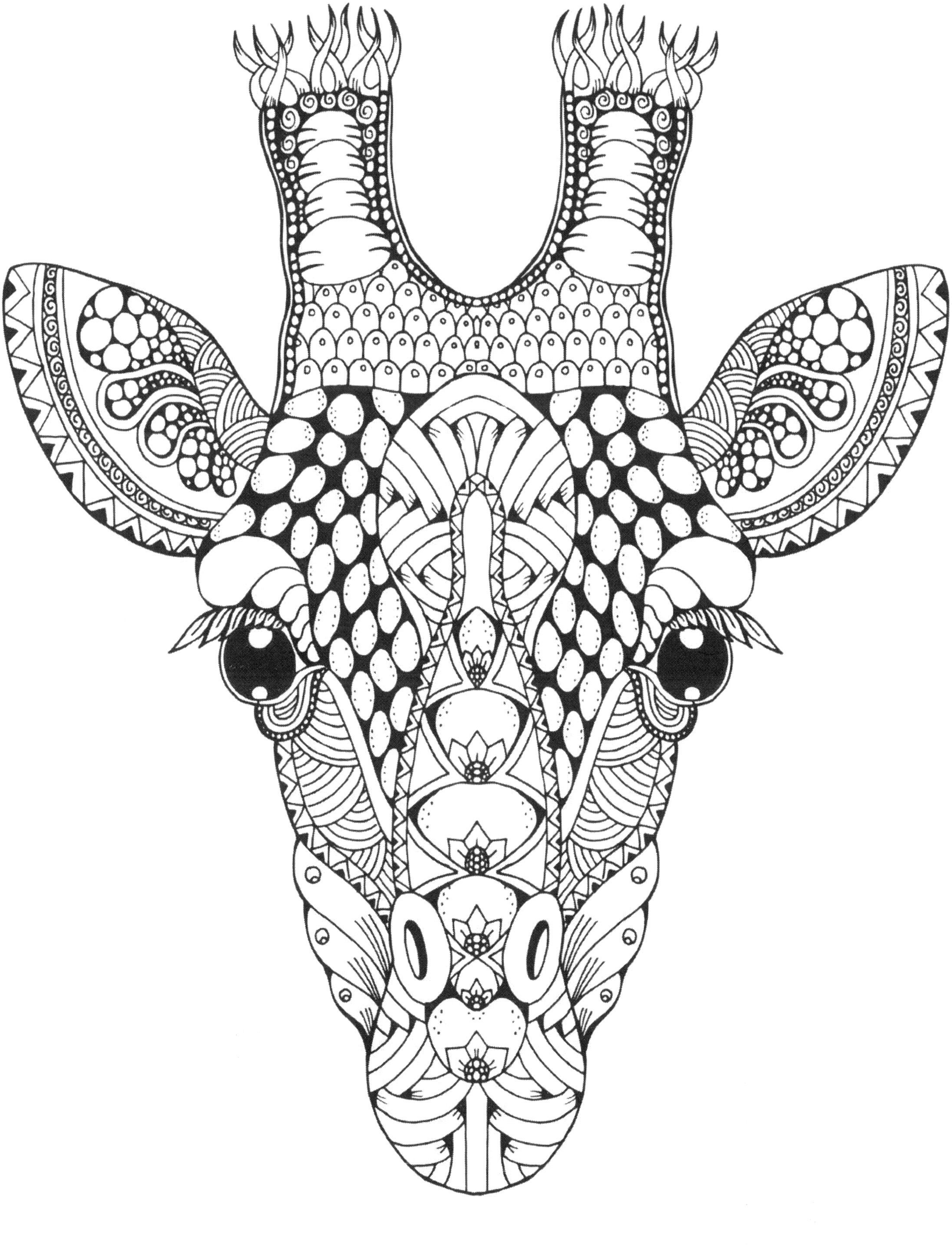

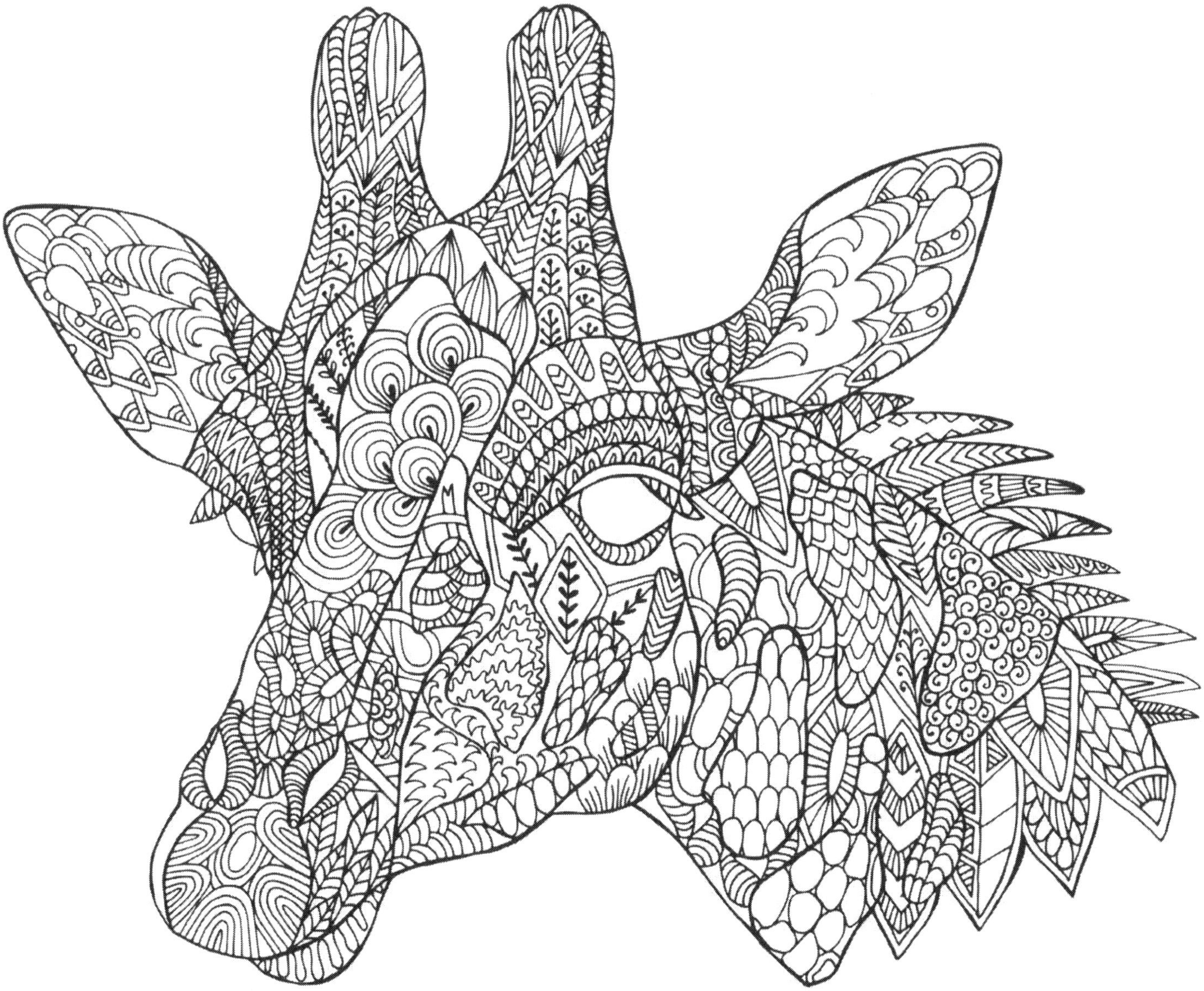

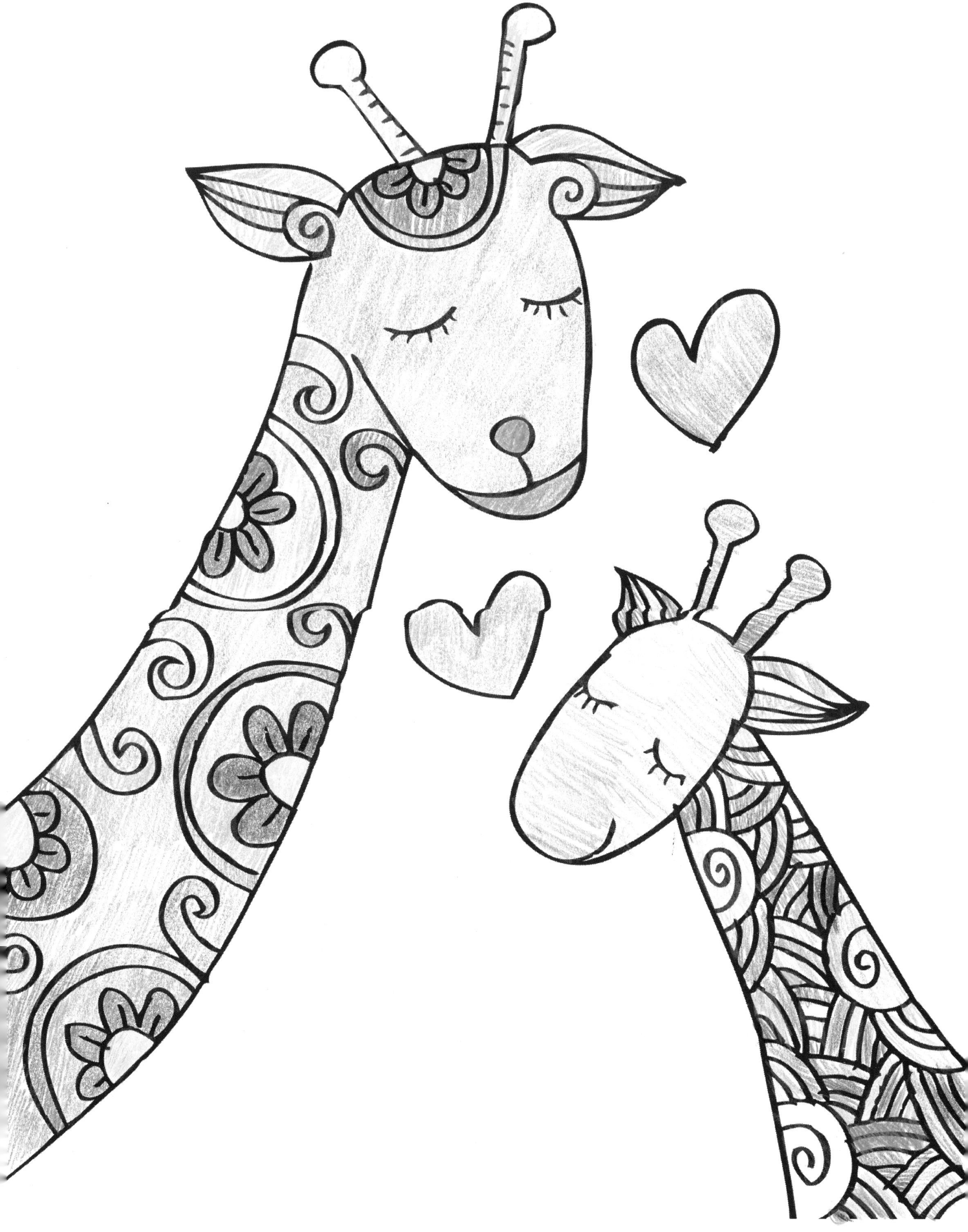

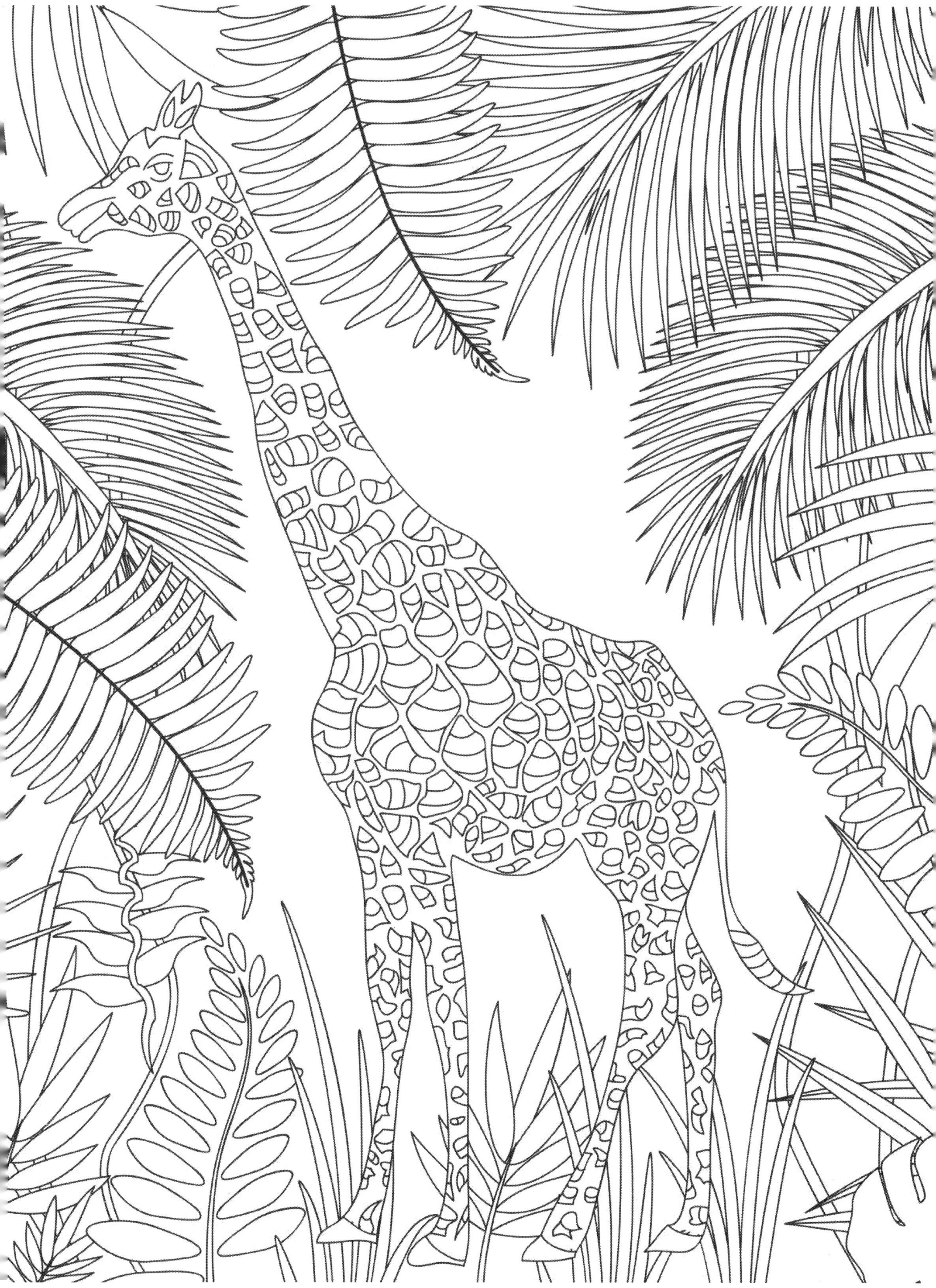

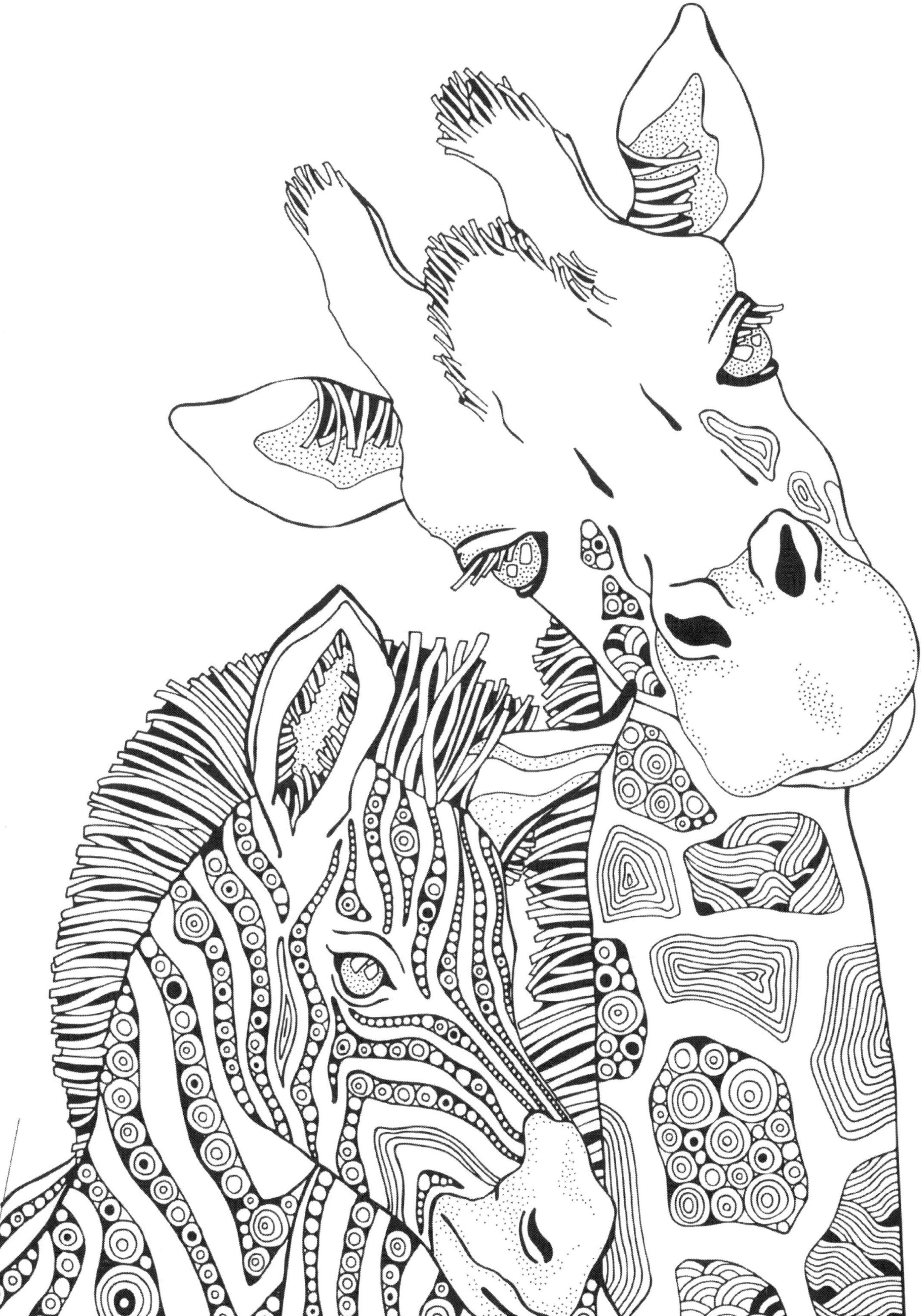

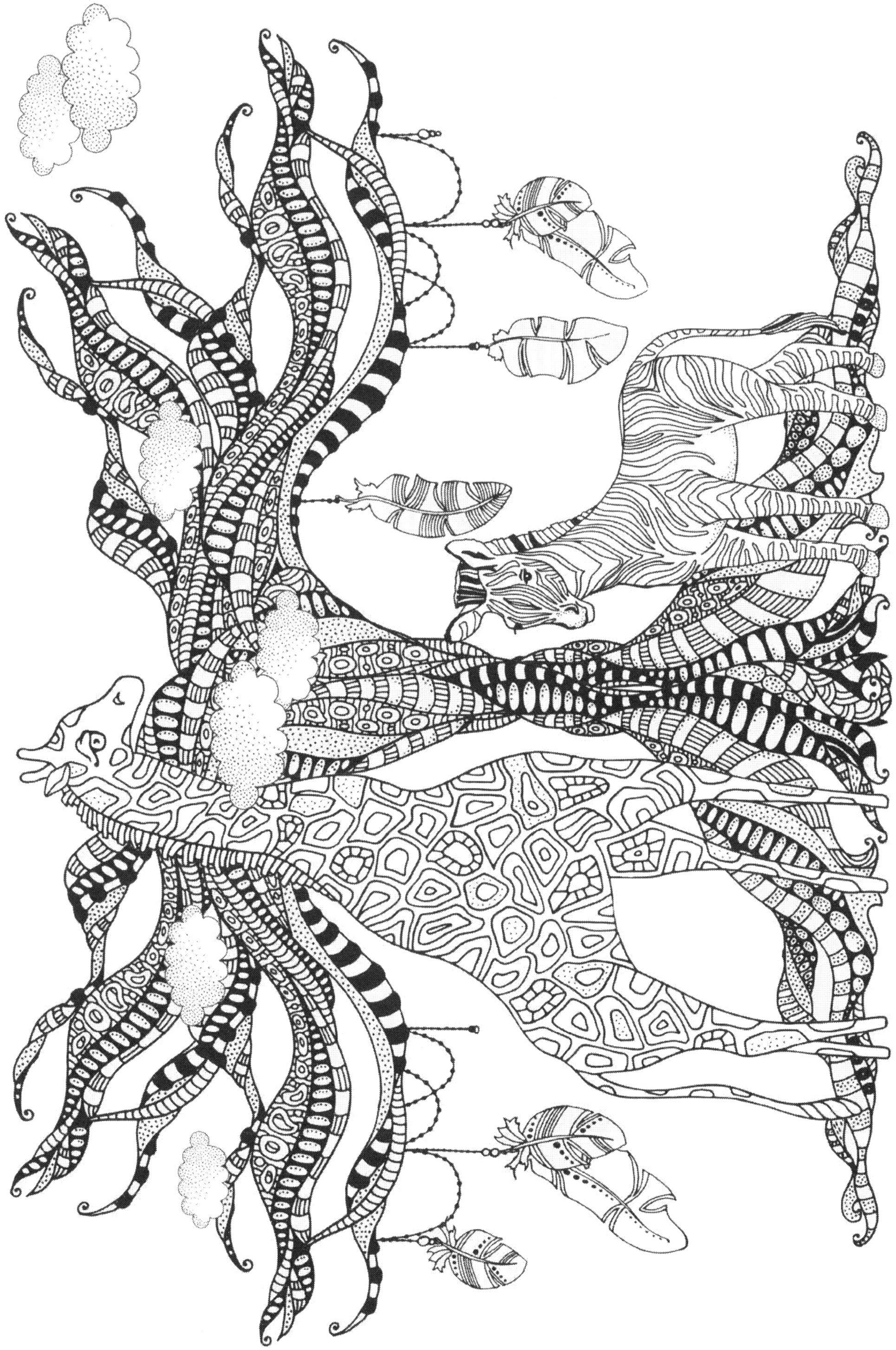

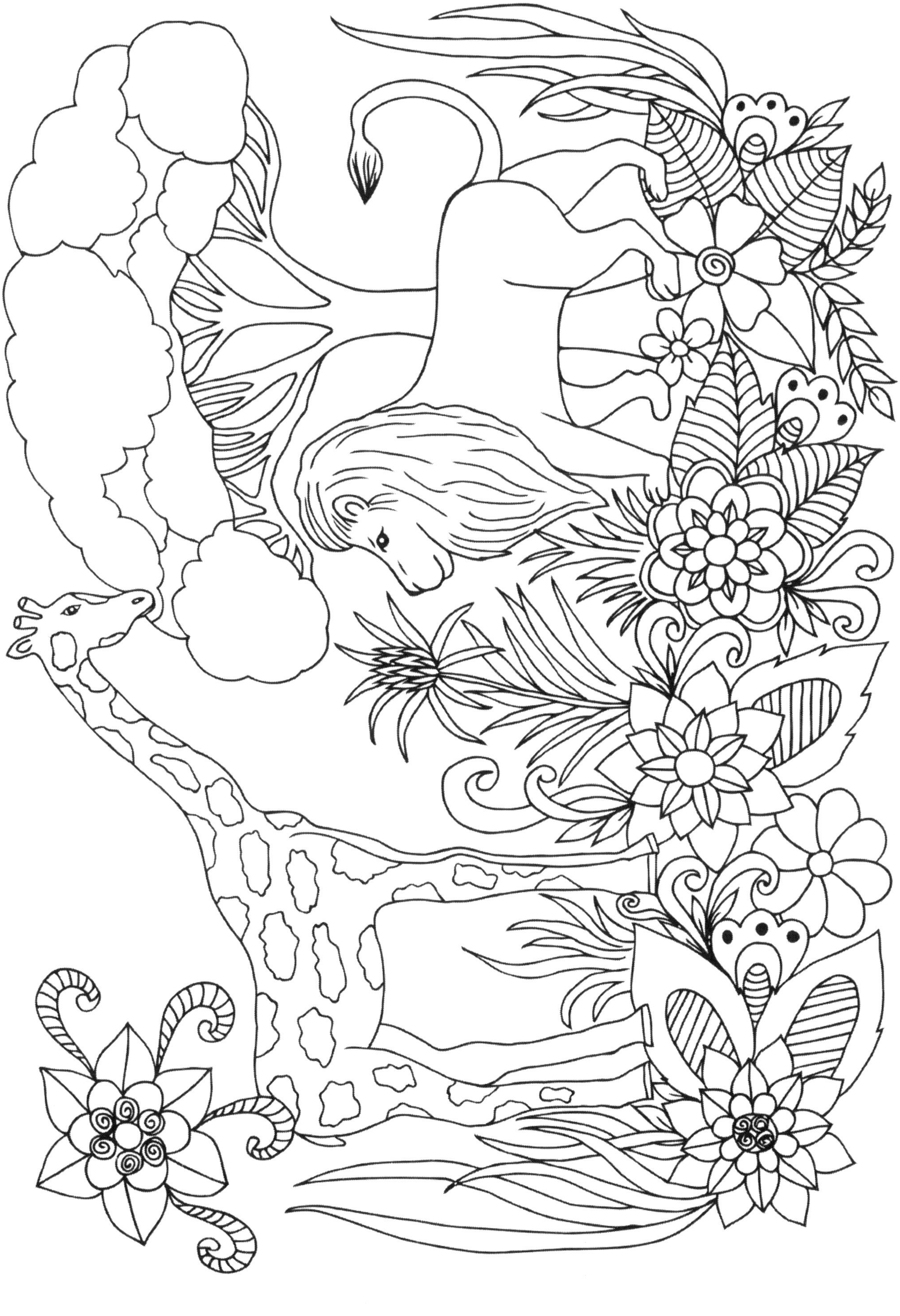

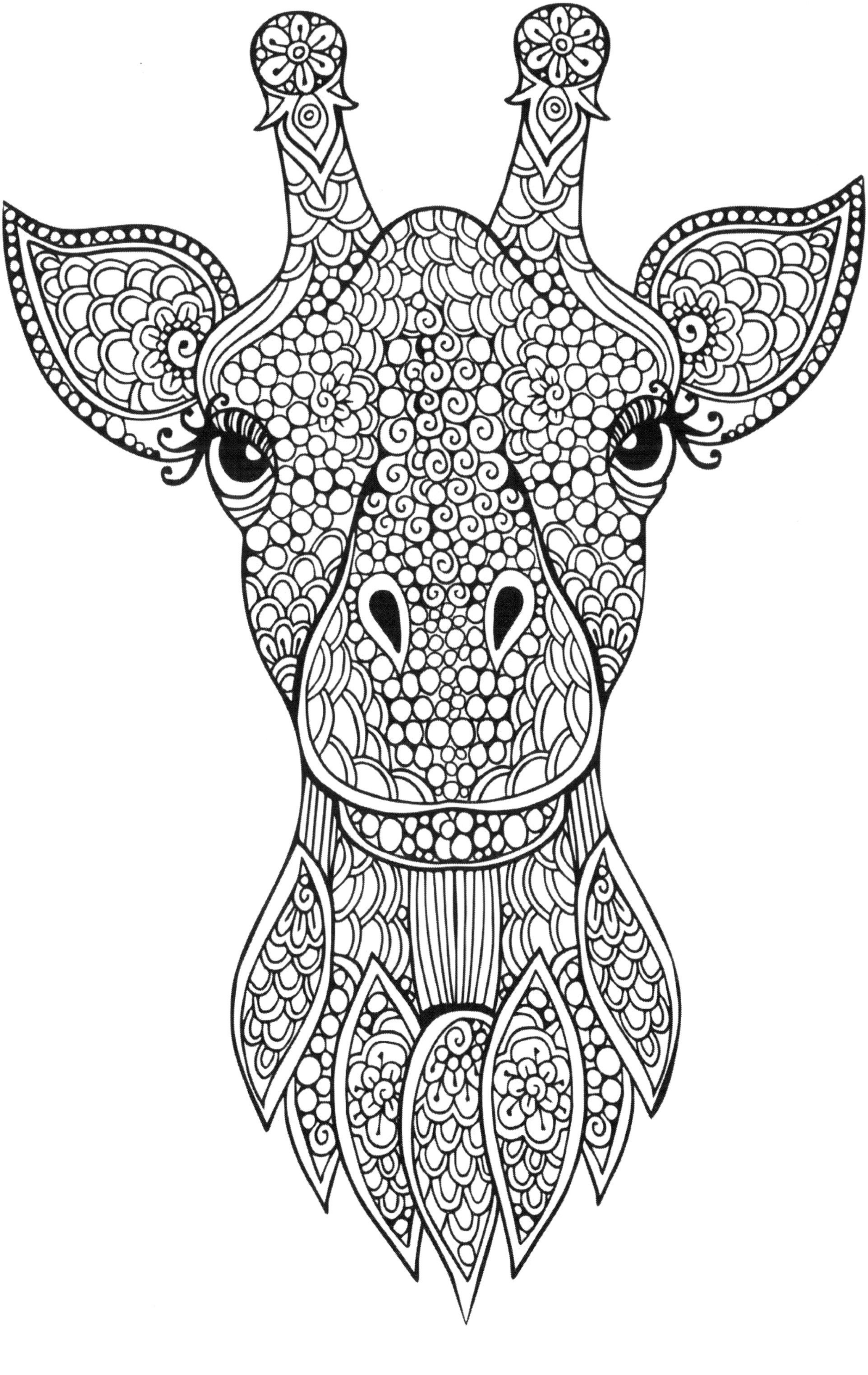

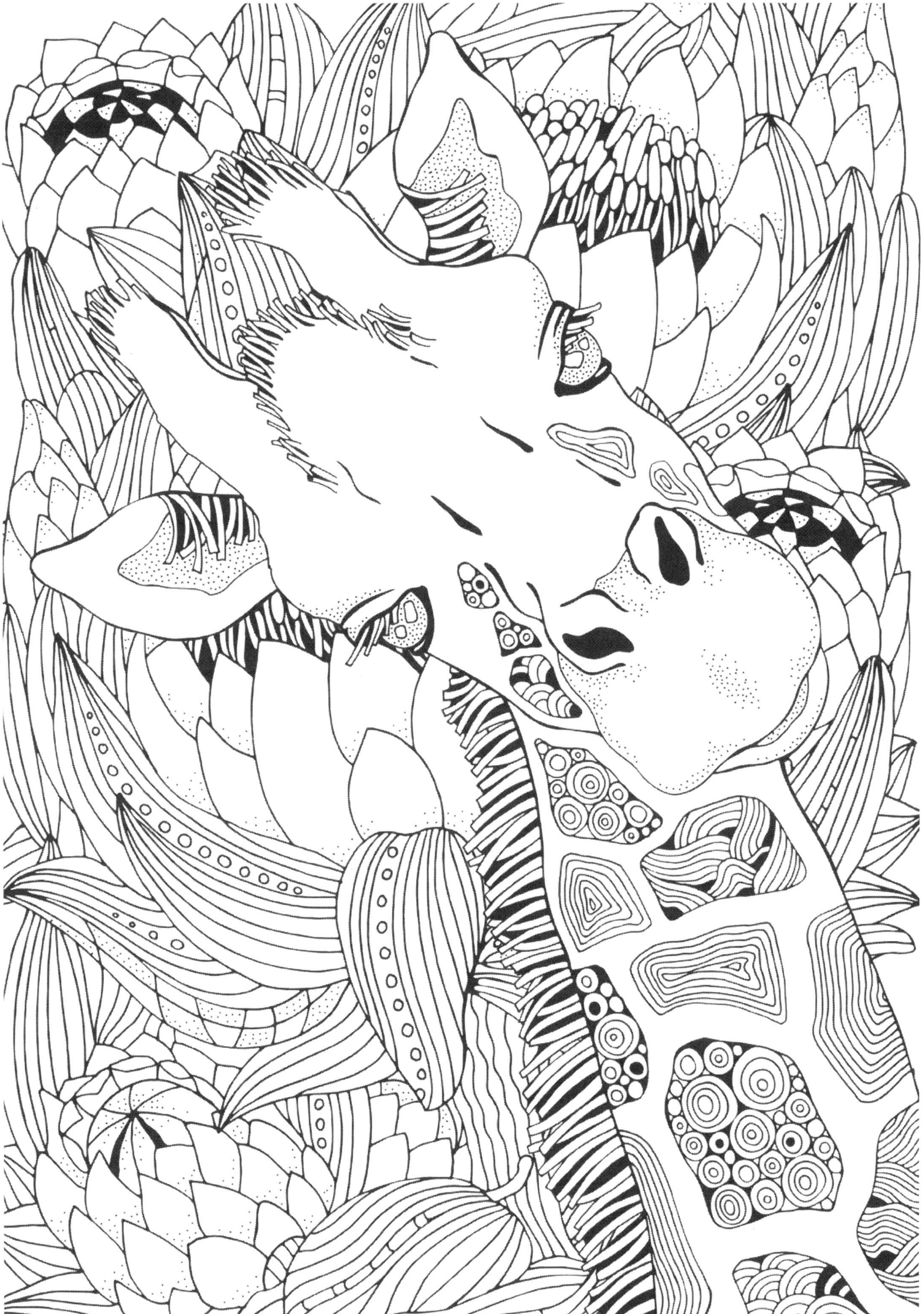

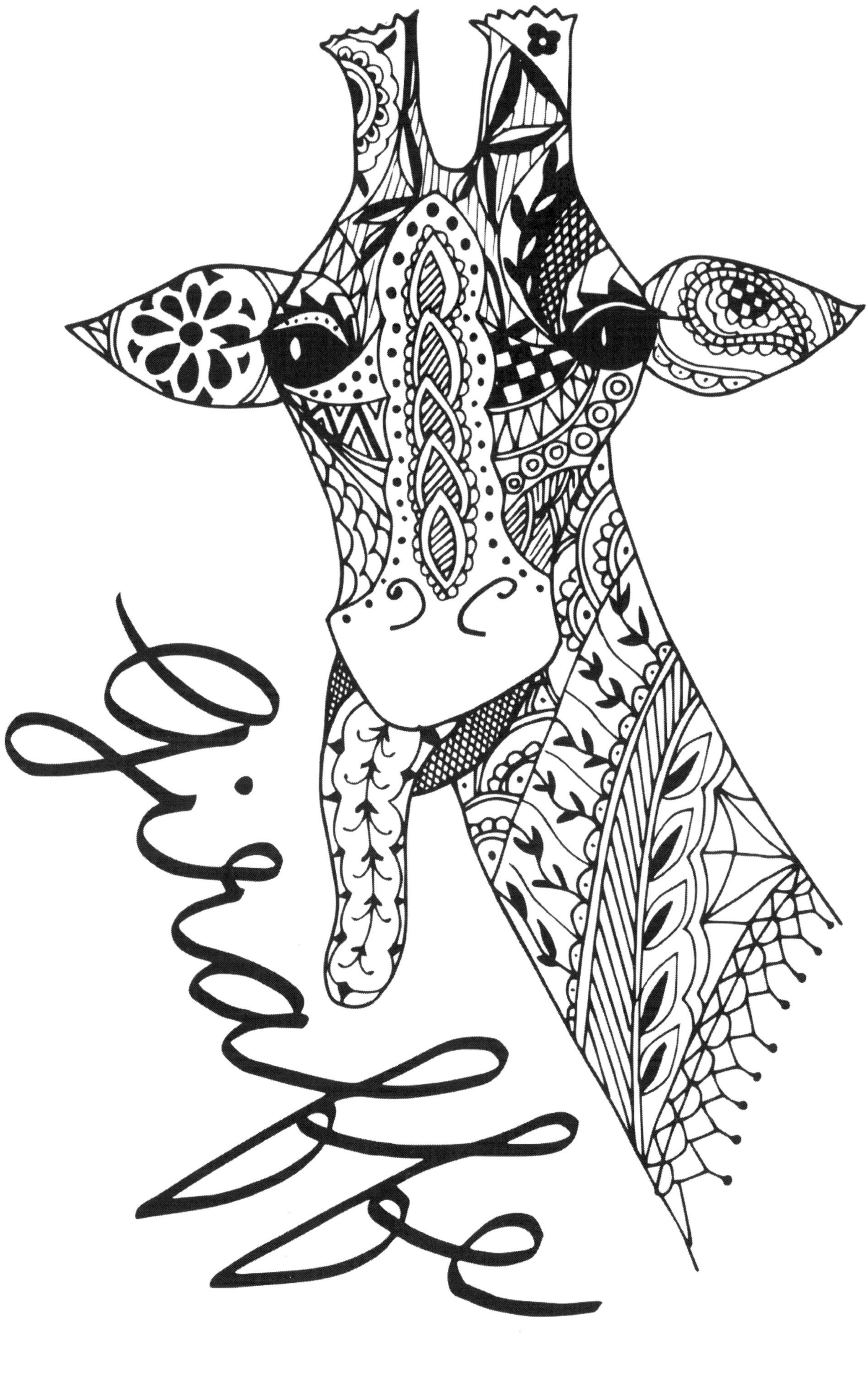
Giraffe

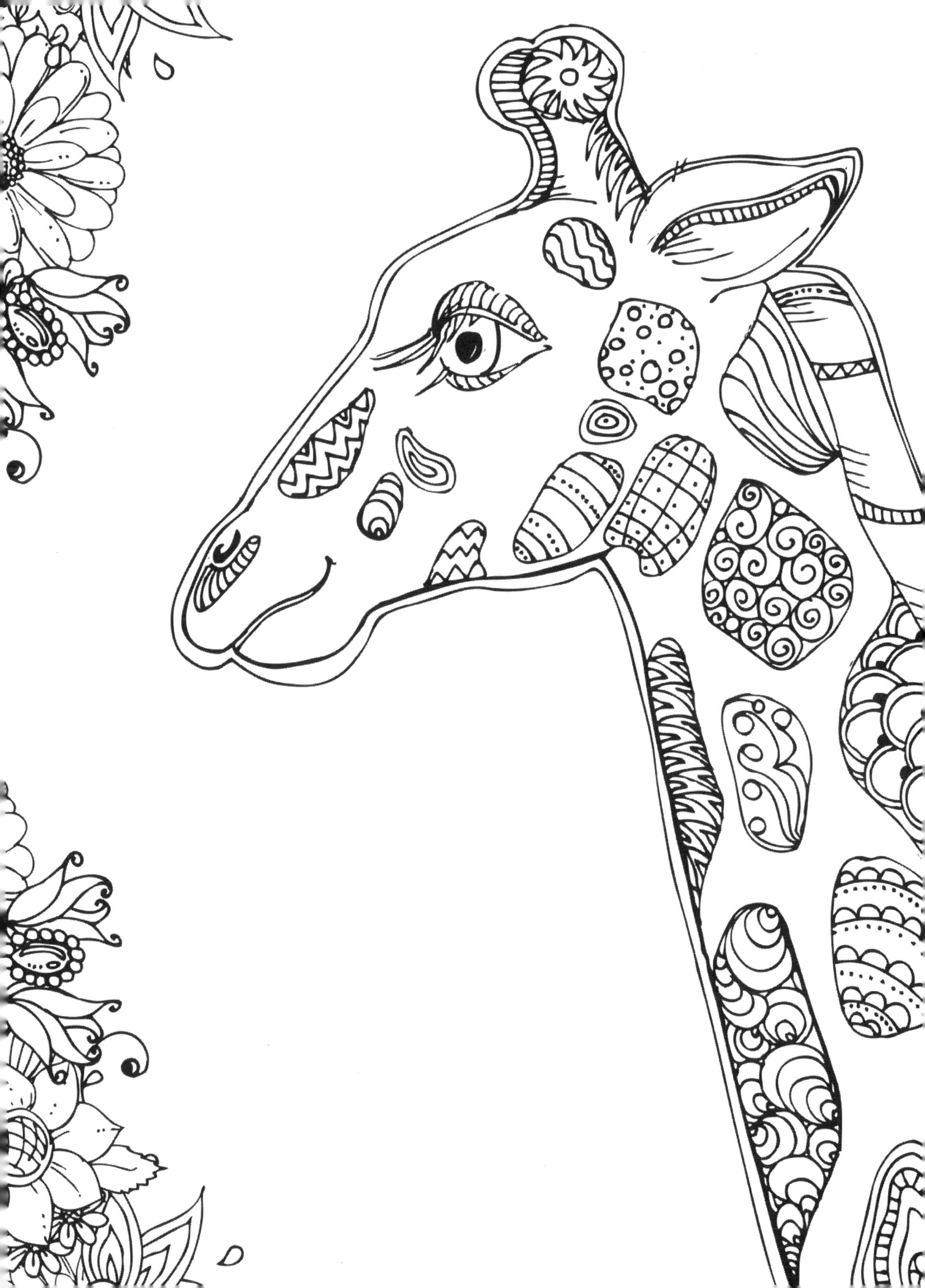

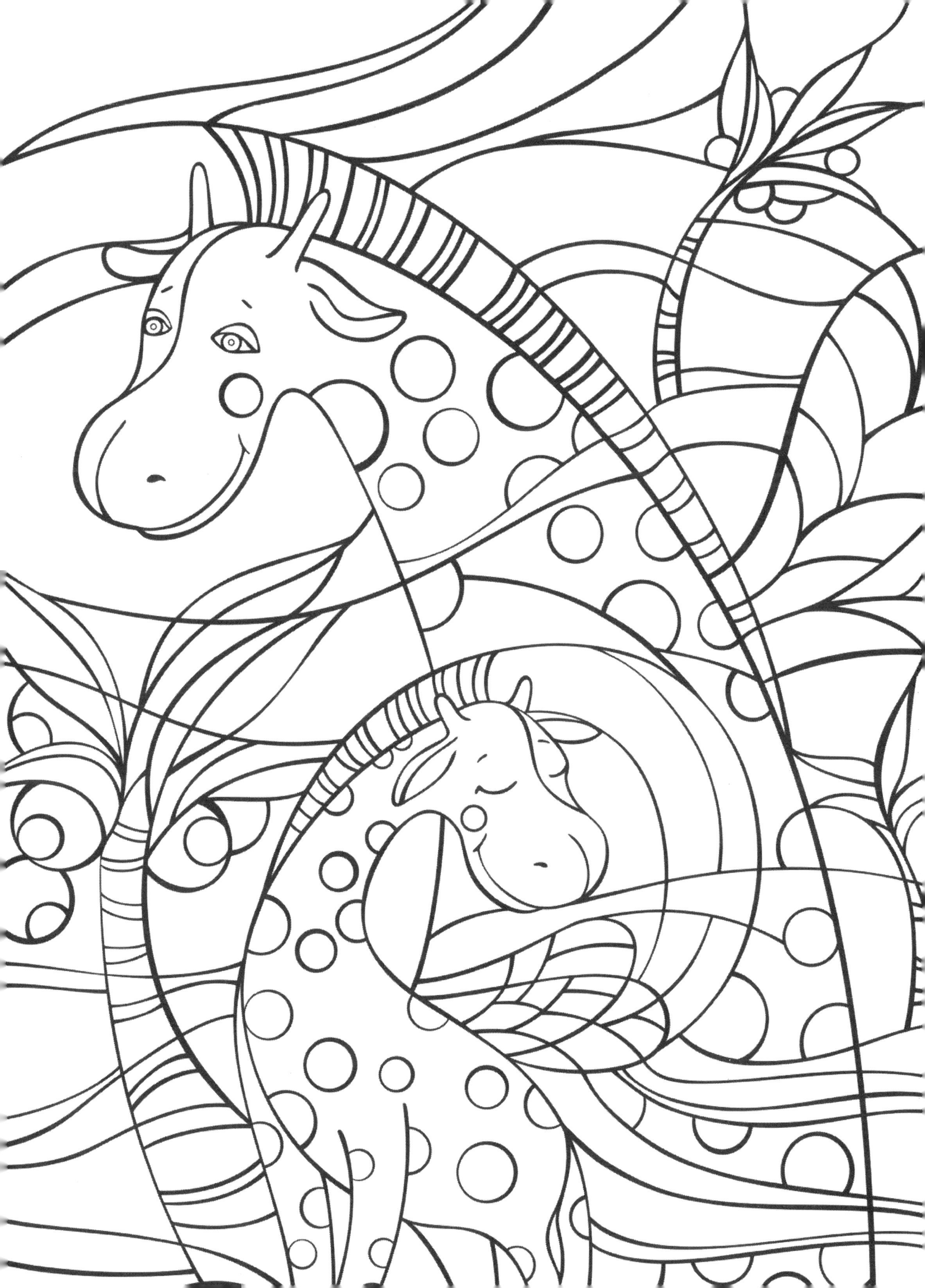

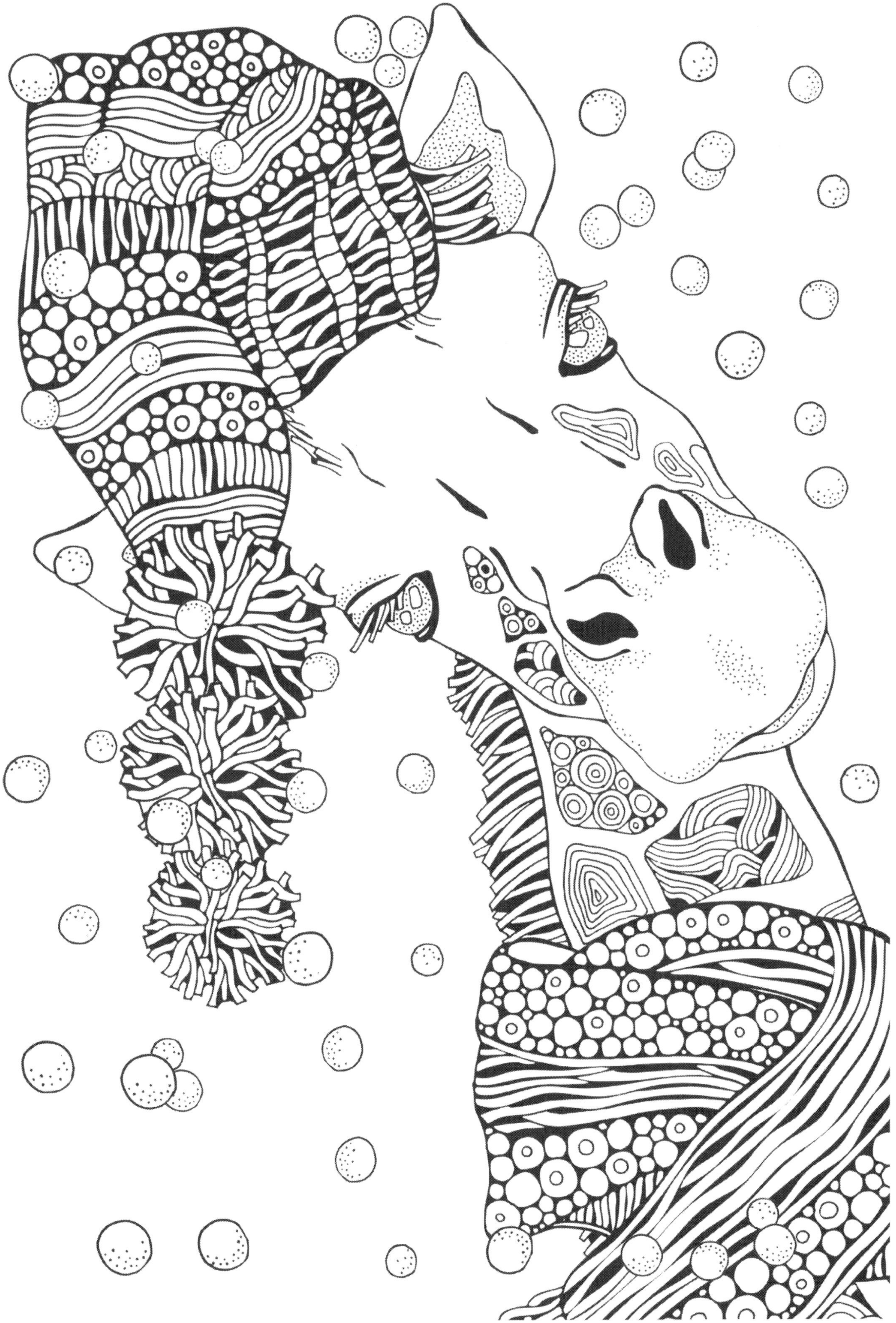

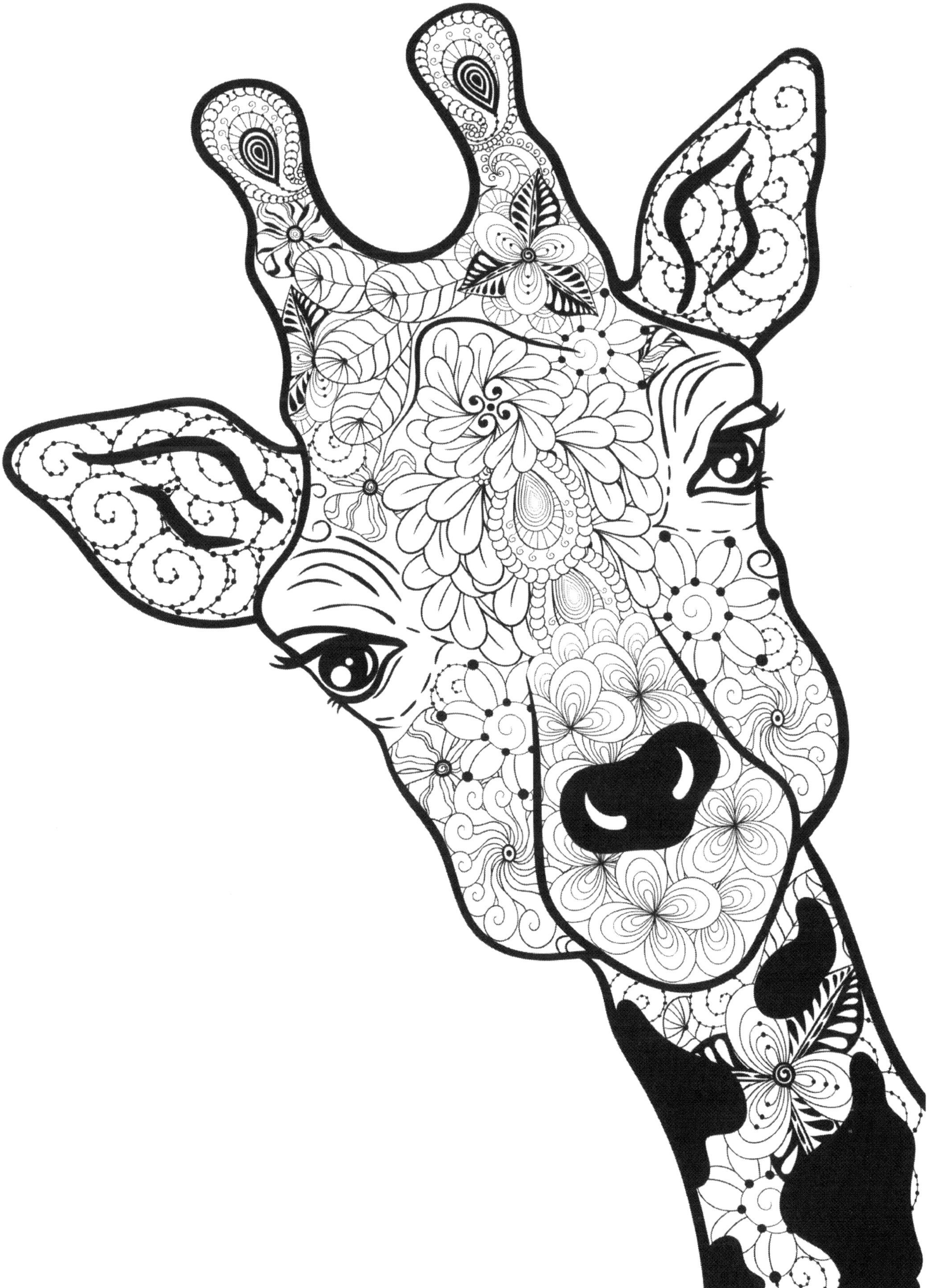

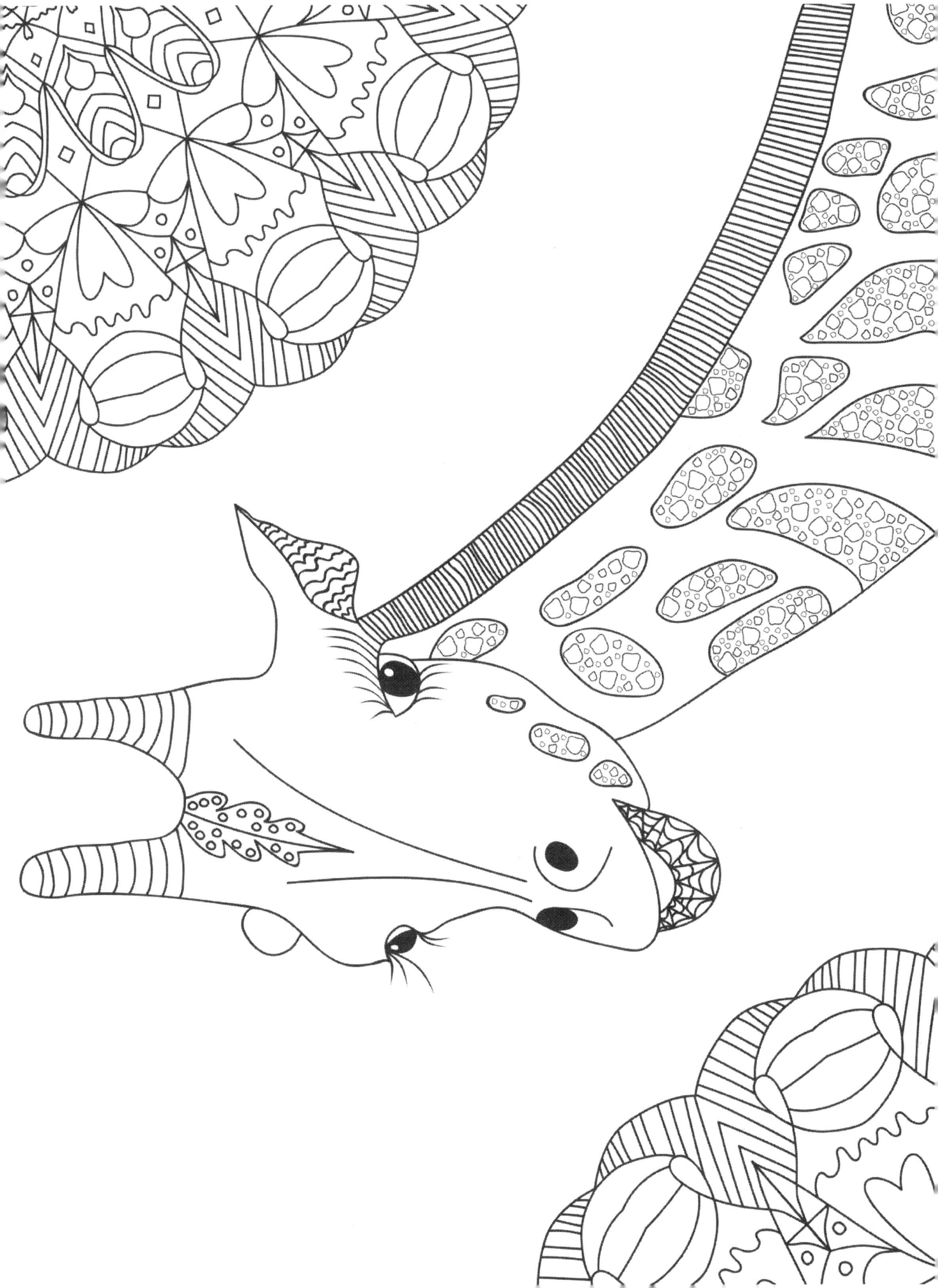

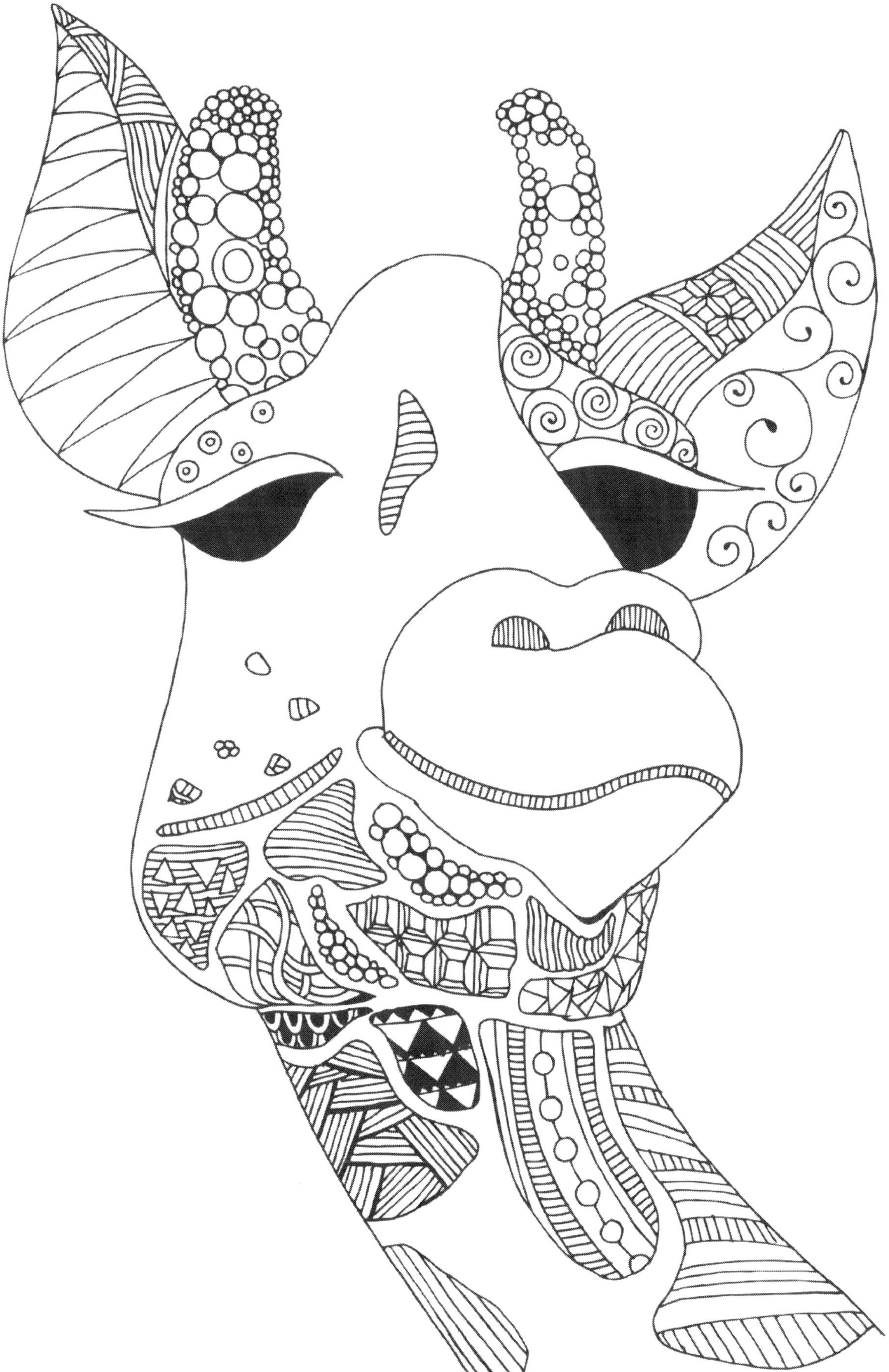

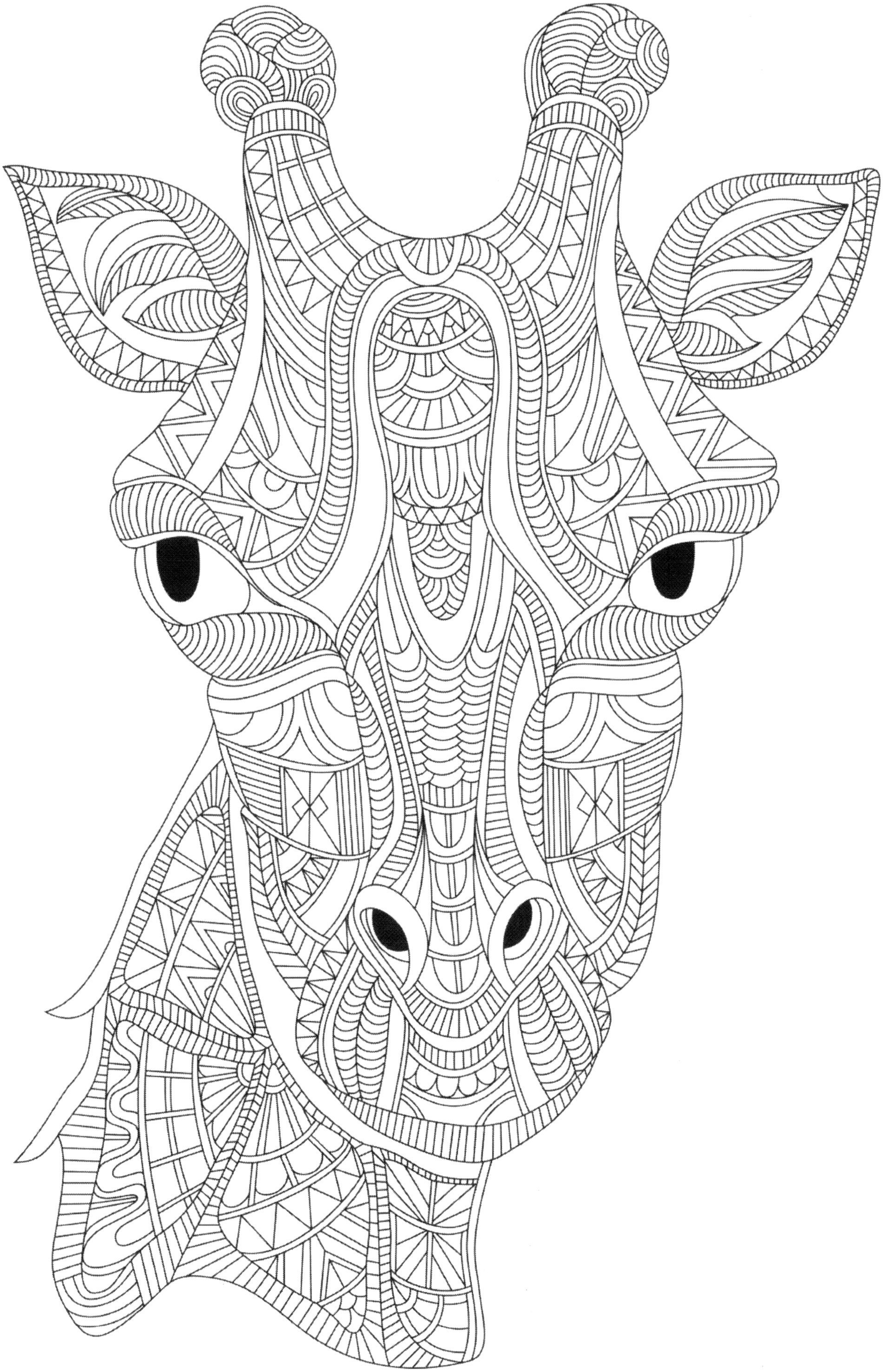

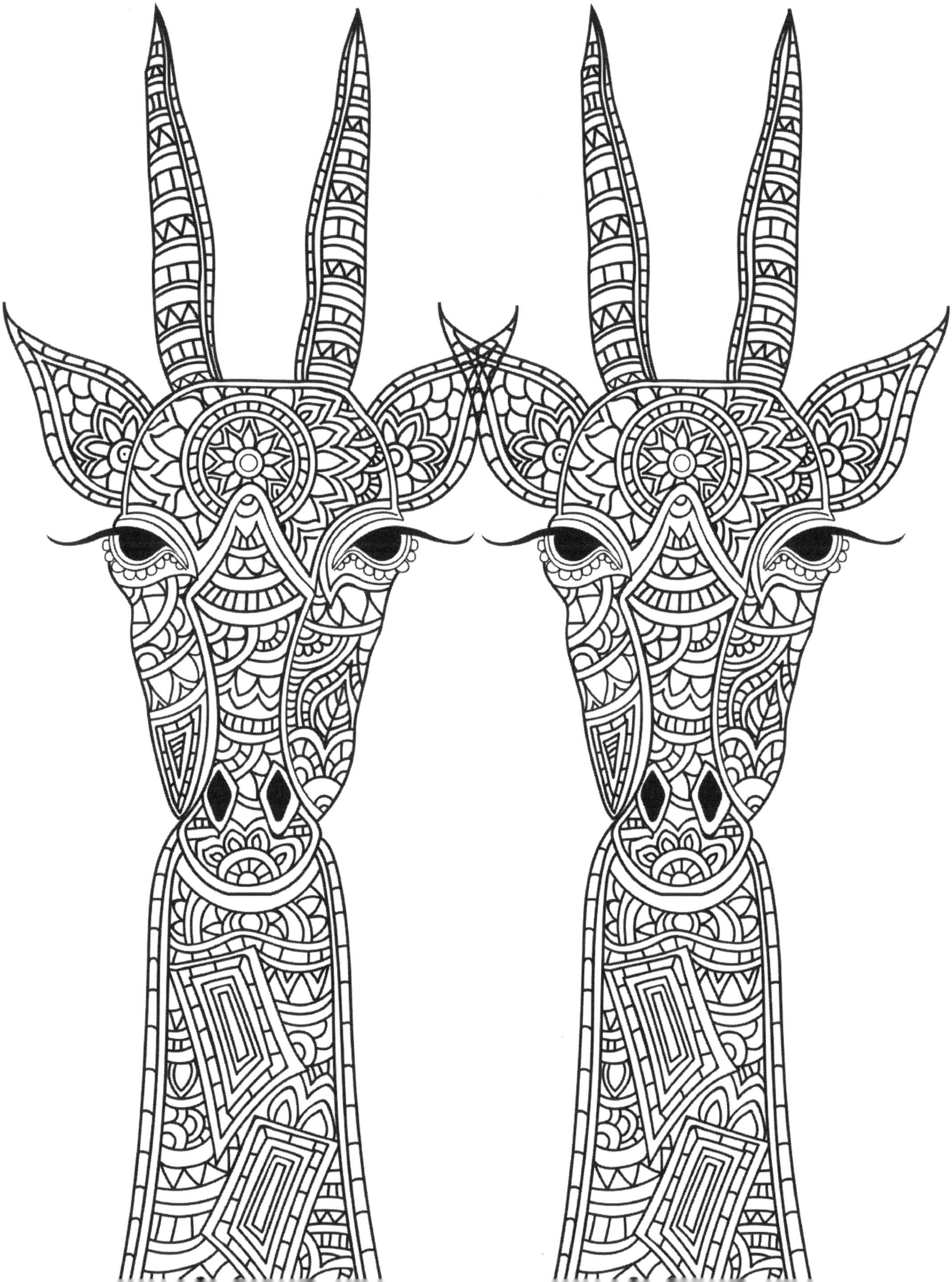

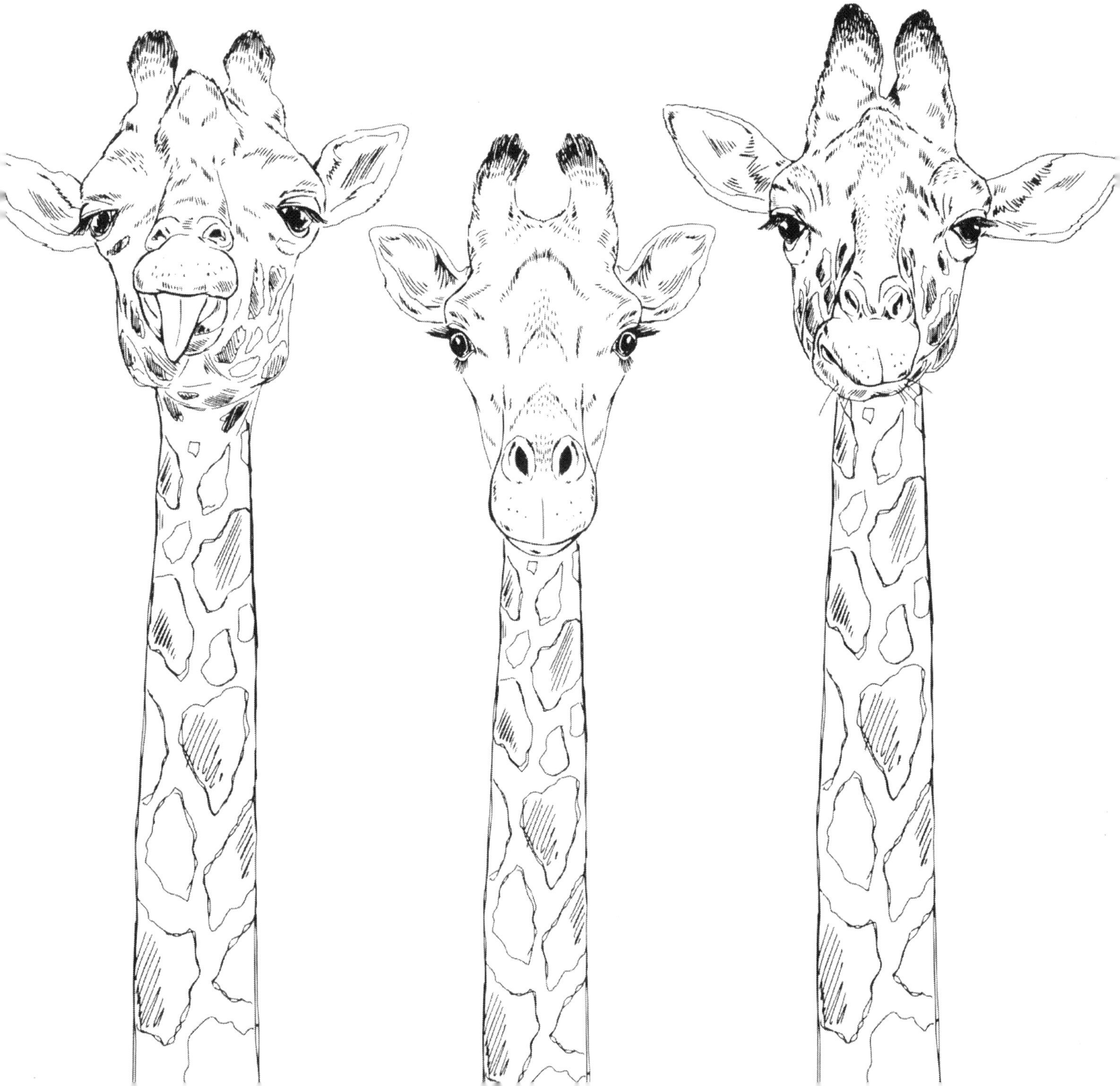

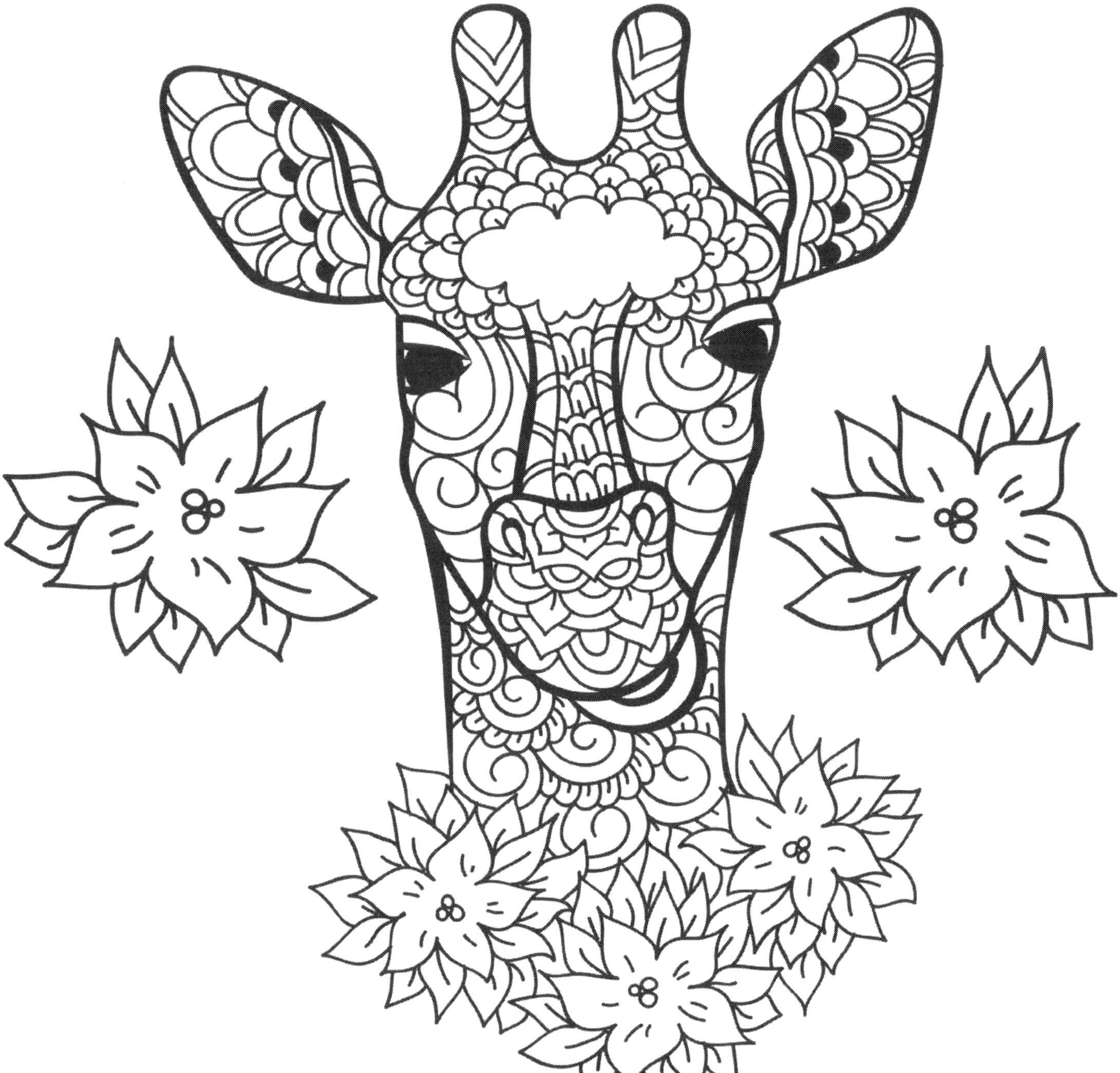

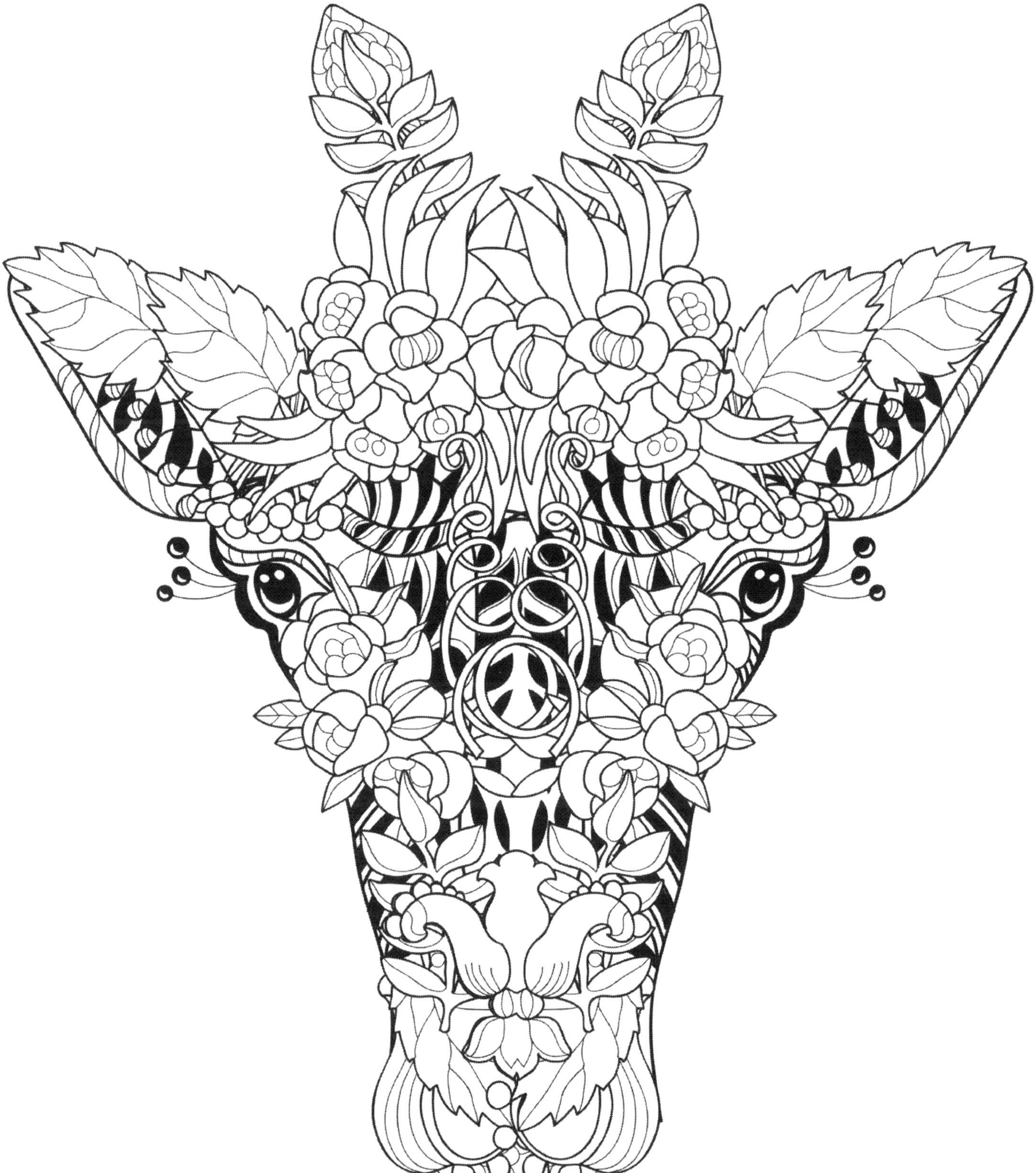

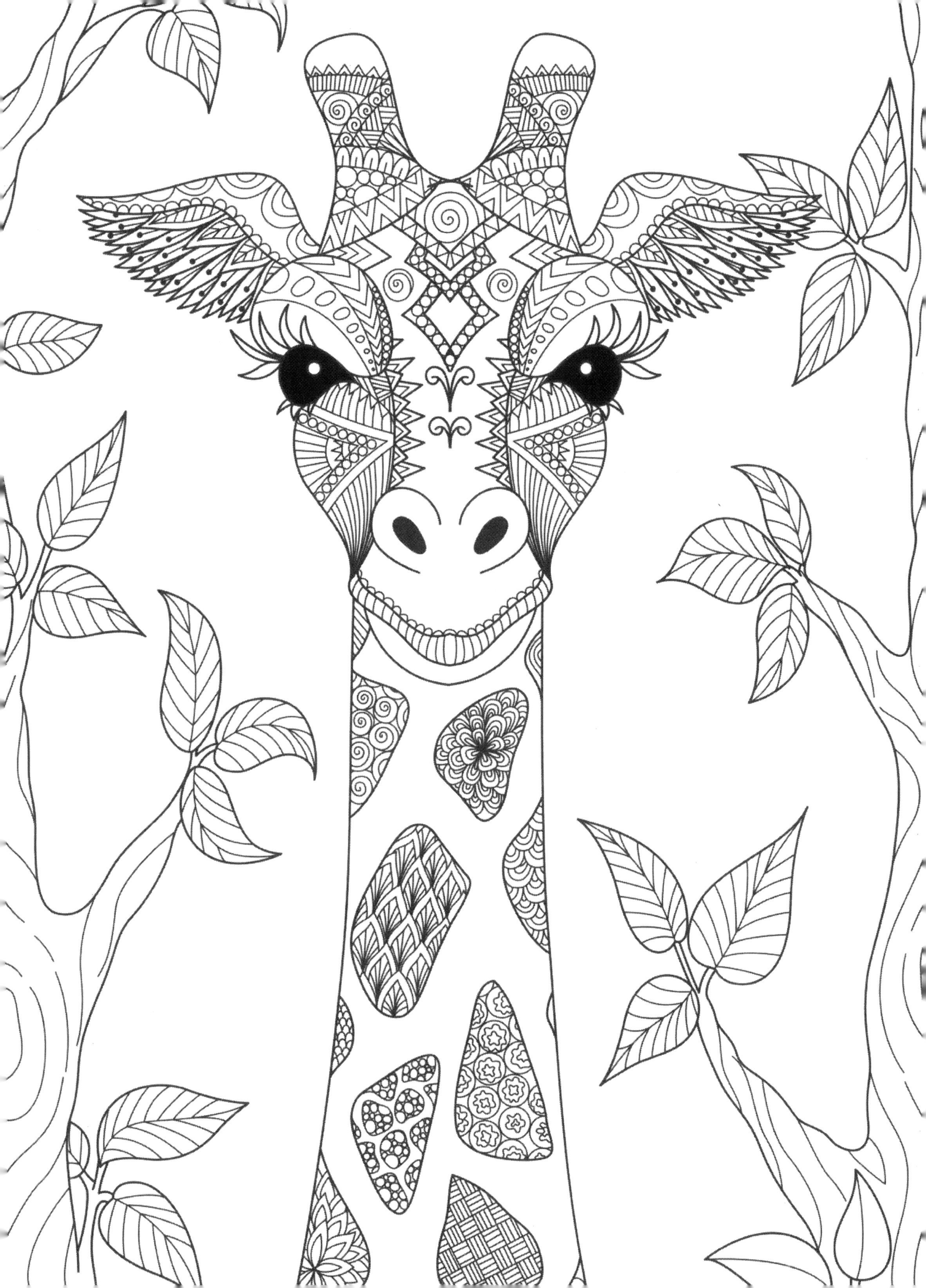

85884890R00033

Made in the USA
San Bernardino, CA
23 August 2018